New Year's Day

Kathryn A. Imler

Heinemann Library
Chicago, Illinois

HEINEMANN-RAINTREE

TO ORDER:

☎ Phone Customer Service **888-454-2279**

💻 Visit **www.heinemannraintree.com** to browse our catalog and order online.

©2008 Heinemann-Raintree
a division of Pearson Education Limited
Chicago, Illinois

Editorial: Rebecca Rissman
Design: Kimberly R. Miracle and Tony Miracle
Picture Research: Kathy Creech and Tracy Cummins
Production: Duncan Gilbert

Originated by Chroma Graphics (Overseas) Pte. Ltd
Printed and bound in China by South China Printing Co. Ltd.
The paper used to print this book comes from sustainable resources.

ISBN-13: 978-1-4329-1043-3 (hc)
ISBN-10: 1-4329-1043-4 (hc)
ISBN-13: 978-1-4329-1051-8 (pb)
ISBN-10: 1-4329-1051-5 (pb)

12 11 10 09 08
10 9 8 7 6 5 4 3 2 1

Library of Congress Cataloging-in-Publication Data
Imler, Kathryn A., 1950-
  New Year's Day / Kathryn A. Imler.
    p. cm. — (Holiday histories)
Summary: A basic introduction to how and why New Year's day is celebrated as a holiday.
Includes bibliographical references and index.
1st Edition ISBN 1-4034-3503-0(HC), 1-4034-3688-6 (Pbk.) 1. New Year—Juvenile literature. [1. New Year. 2. Holidays.] I. Title. II. Series.
  GT4905.I553 2003
  394.2614—dc21
                              2003007828

Acknowledgments
The author and publishers are grateful to the following for permission to reproduce copyright material: **p. 4** ©Mike Segar/Reuters Photo Archive/NewsCom; **p. 5** ©Touhig Sion/Corbis SYGMA; **p. 6** ©Christie's Images/Corbis; **pp. 7, 20** ©Mary Evans Picture Library; **pp. 8, 14, 15, 16** ©Hulton Archive/Getty Images; **p. 9** ©Corbis; **pp. 10, 11, 12** ©Bettmann/Corbis; **p. 12** ©Erich Lessing/Art Resource, NY; **p. 17** ©Reuters News Picture Service; **p. 18** ©North Wind Picture Archives; **p. 19** ©PhotoDisc/Getty Images; **p. 21** ©Samba Images/Getty Images; **p. 22** ©Anne Ackermann/Getty Images; **p. 23** ©Digital Vision/Getty Images; **p. 24** ©Mark Lennihan/AP Wide World Photo; **p. 25** ©Kathy Willen/AP Wide World Photo; **p. 26** ©Photodisc Green/Getty Images; **p. 27** ©Nick Ut/AP Wide World Photos; **p. 28** ©Britt Erlanson/Getty Images; **p. 29** ©Reuters Photo Archive/NewsCom

Cover photograph reproduced with the permission of ©istockphoto/Skip ODonnell

Contents

Some words are shown in bold, **like this**. You can find out what they mean by looking in the glossary.

A Fresh Start

Everyone watches the clock. At exactly midnight, horns blow, people shout and cheer. Bells ring in the first day of the new year.

On New Year's Day, people relax. Parades and football games are on television. Families and friends visit. They greet each other and call out, "Happy New Year!"

Marking Time

Long ago, people did not have clocks. They were able to tell time by using things that happened in nature. People marked each day by the sunrise and sunset.

A new moon appeared about every thirty days. This was how a month was marked. People looked to nature for a sign of the new year, too.

Beginnings and Endings

In some places, people would end their year when it was time to **harvest** their crops. A harvest day was New Year's Day.

This is a picture of the Nile River in Egypt.
The Nile River is the longest river in the world.

In ancient Egypt, New Year's Day was the day the Nile River flooded. That was the beginning of Egypt's planting season and its new year.

This is a drawing of a Roman banquet. Romans often had banquets, or large dinners, to celebrate the New Year.

The Roman Calendar

Later, many **ancient** people chose March to start a new year. They chose March because it was spring. In spring it was easy to start growing things. They had **festivals** to celebrate the new year.

Julius Caesar was a Roman emperor. An emperor was ruler of a large group of countries.

But Roman **emperors** liked changing dates. They did not care about the moon or growing seasons. Julius Caesar tried to stop these changes. He **declared** January 1 the start of the new year.

How January Got Its Name

The Romans believed in many different gods. Each god had a special job. One god they belived in was Janus. Janus had two faces.

This painting shows different Roman gods.

JANUS.

One face watched who went out. The other face watched who came in. The word for January came from his name. One face looks backward to the past year. One looks ahead to the new year.

Lots of Calendars

Hundreds of years after the Romans, people lived in many places. They did not all follow the Roman calendar. Countries such as Spain and Germany started the new year on Christmas Day.

This drawing shows people enjoying a spring celebration.

Italy and France still thought March was the best time. Other countries chose Easter to start their new year.

Back to January

In the 1600s, a **pope** named Gregory fixed the calendar. He **declared** January 1 New Year's Day again. Many countries followed this calendar.

GREGORIVS XIII. *Hugo Boncom*

But not everyone. Even today, the Chinese New Year is different. It comes at the end of January or in February. The Jewish New Year is in the Fall.

The Colonies Catch Up

England and its **colonies** kept their own calendar
for a long time. Until 1752, England and its colonies
began the new year on March 25.

Later, England changed its new year to January 1. The colonies broke away from England. The colonies became the United States of America. America changed its new year to January 1, too.

A Noisy Night

Ancient people in China believed that evil spirits came out around the new year. They thought the spirits brought bad luck. They tried to scare them away with lots of noise.

On New Year's Eve, people still do this. Maybe they do not believe in evil spirits. But they make noise. They shoot off fireworks.

Out with the Old

There are many **customs** for saying goodbye to the old year. You may be invited to a big party.

Or you might stay home and watch a movie.

In with the New

The United States starts the new year in a special way. People wait for the last seconds before midnight. They count down, "10...9...8...." At midnight, a huge **glittering** ball drops down a pole.

This **custom** has been around for almost one hundred years. It happens in New York City. But people watch it on television all over the country. People all over the world wait to see it.

Some Traditions

Visiting friends on New Year's Day is an old **custom**. Some people fix special foods. Some people believe that if you eat black-eyed peas or roast pork on New Year's Day you will have good luck.

The Tournament of Roses Parade has been around since 1890. Everyone likes seeing the colorful floats. They like watching football, too.

Looking Ahead

When starting a new year people often think about the past. They think about making **resolutions**.

We say goodbye to the old year. We say hello to the new one. We hope for good things to come.

Important Dates

New Year's Day

10,000 B.C.E.	The first calendar is developed using the moon. A month is calculated by the appearance of a new moon
45 C.E.	Julius Caesar declares January 1 New Year's Day
1200	Many European countries have different days for New Year's Day
1582	Pope Gregory XIII re-declares January 1 as New Year's Day
1752	England and its colonies in America move New Year's Day to January 1
January 1, 1890	First Tournament of Roses Parade is in Pasadena, California
December 31, 1907	First New Year's Eve ball is dropped at Times Square in New York

Glossary

colony group of people who live in a new land

custom something people have done the same way for a long time

declare officially say something is so

emperor ruler of a large group of countries

harvest season that crops are gathered

glitter shiny

pope head of the Catholic Church

resolution promise

Find Out More

Hughes, Monica. *My Chinese New Year.* Chicago: Raintree, 2006.

Rau, Dana Meachen. *New Year's Day.* New York: Children's Press, 2000.

Schuh, Mari C. *Let's Find Out About New Year's Day.* Bloomington, MN: Pebble Books, 2002.

Index